The Stamp Act of 1765

The Stamp Act of 1765

Dennis Brindell Fradin

Marshall Cavendish
Benchmark
New York

Marshall Cavendish Benchmark
99 White Plains Road
Tarrytown, NY 10591
www.marshallcavendish.us

Text and map copyright © 2010 by Marshall Cavendish Corporation
Map by XNR Productions

All Internet sites were available and accurate when sent to press.

Library of Congress Cataloging-in-Publication Data

Fradin, Dennis B.
The Stamp Act of 1765 / by Dennis Brindell Fradin.
p. cm. — (Turning points in U.S. history)
Includes bibliographical references and index.
Summary: "Covers the Stamp Act of 1765 as a watershed event in U.S. history, influencing social, economic,
and political policies that shaped the nation's future"—Provided by publisher.
ISBN 978-0-7614-4260-8
1. Great Britain. Stamp Act (1765)—Juvenile literature. 2. Taxation--Political aspects—United States—History—18th century—Juvenile literature.
3. Protest movements—United States—History—18th century—Juvenile literature. 4. Riots—United States—History—18th century—Juvenile literature.
5. United States—History—Revolution, 1775-1783—Causes—Juvenile literature. I. Title.
E215.2.F73 2009
973.3'111—dc22
2008028365

Photo Research by Connie Gardner
Cover Photo: The Granger Collection
Cover: A nineteenth-century colored engraving depicts the Sons of Liberty marching with an effigy of a stamp master.
Title Page: A cartoon protesting the Stamp Act, printed in the *Philadelphia Journal*, 1765

The photographs in this book are used by permission and through the courtesy of: *The Granger Collection:* 3, 9(B),16, 20, 25, 26, 20, 36; *Art Resource, NY:* 6;
Art Archive: Culver Pictures, 9(T); Gripsholm Castle, Sweden/Alfredo Dagli Orti, 17; *North Wind Picture Archives:* 10, 13, 14, 22, 24, 34, 40-41; *Bridgeman Art
Library:* Colonel Issac Barre, 1785 (oil on canvas), 19; *Corbis:* Bettmann, 30; *Alamy:* North Wind Picture Archives, 32.
Timeline: North Wind Picture Archives.

Editor: Deborah Grahame
Publisher: Michelle Bisson
Art Director: Anahid Hamparian
Printed in Malaysia
1 3 5 6 4 2

Contents

This painting depicts Fort James at Jamestown, Virginia, in 1607.

CHAPTER ONE

England's Thirteen American Colonies

By the 1600s, several European nations wanted to rule the area that became the United States. France and Spain established **colonies** in the region. The Netherlands and Sweden also founded colonies. England had the most success at colonizing America, however. England founded Virginia, its first American colony, in 1607. The colony of Georgia followed in 1733. Between these two dates, England founded or took control of eleven other American colonies.

For many years, the colonists were loyal to the Mother Country, as they called England. For example, England fought France for control of North America from 1754 to 1763. Because thousands of Native Americans

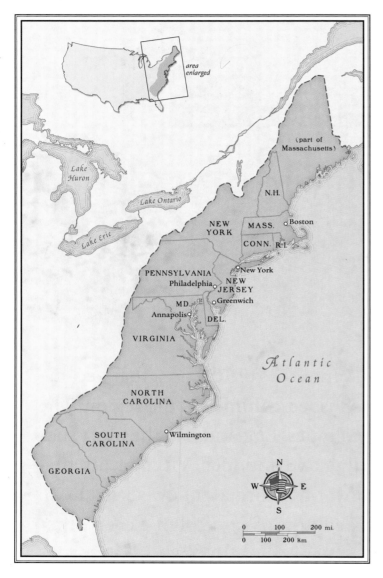

The original thirteen colonies, settled between 1607 and 1733.

fought on France's side, this conflict was called the French and Indian War. England had help, too—from its American colonists. Thanks partly to the Americans, England won the French and Indian War in 1763. England then took over most of France's North American territory.

England had won the French and Indian War, but the British government had a major problem. The war had been costly, and the Mother Country was deeply in **debt**. By 1764, England's national debt was 130 million pounds. That would equal billions of American dollars today. People in England already paid high taxes, so squeezing more money out of them would be difficult. How would England obtain the money to pay its bills?

A British general leads the redcoats into battle during the French and Indian War.

George Grenville (1712–1770)

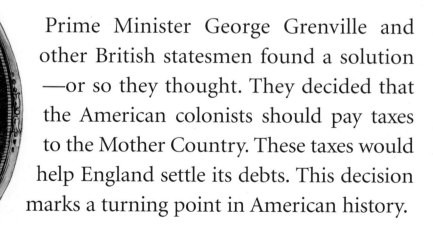

Prime Minister George Grenville and other British statesmen found a solution —or so they thought. They decided that the American colonists should pay taxes to the Mother Country. These taxes would help England settle its debts. This decision marks a turning point in American history.

King George presides over the House of Commons in the British Parliament.

CHAPTER TWO

A Taxing Situation

In early 1765, Britain's **Parliament**, or lawmaking body, passed its first major tax on the Americans. It was called the Stamp Act. The new law required the colonists to buy special tax stamps. The stamps would be used on a variety of paper goods.

Colonists had to buy tax stamps with their newspapers. They also needed stamps for wills and other legal documents. Papers of ships, bills of sale, licenses, pamphlets, advertisements, almanacs, and calendars also required the special stamps. Even packs of playing cards and school diplomas were supposed to have stamps. The Mother Country showed that it meant business about the new law. Forging, or **counterfeiting**, tax stamps was a crime punishable by death.

Note King George's motto, *Honi soit qui mal y pense* (Old French for "Shame on him who thinks evil on it"), and the price of the stamp (one shilling) on these examples of stamps.

Word of the Stamp Act reached the thirteen colonies in April. There was one piece of good news for the Americans. The Stamp Act was not scheduled to take effect until November 1, 1765. That gave the colonists half a year to show what they thought of the new tax law.

What Is a Colony?

A colony is a settlement built by a country beyond its borders. It is ruled by the parent country and often populated by people from the parent country. A country or nation, on the other hand, governs itself and makes its own laws.

Colonists build a spectacular bonfire as they destroy a carriage and other goods during a demonstration against the Stamp Act.

CHAPTER THREE

"Taxation without Representation Is Tyranny!"

When the colonists heard about the Stamp Act, they were enraged. They felt that England should thank them for helping to win the French and Indian War. Instead, the Mother Country was trying to make them pay for the war.

Americans in all thirteen colonies protested. They spoke, wrote, and demonstrated against the Stamp Act.

In Massachusetts, lawyer and politician James Otis spoke out against the new law. "Taxation without representation is **tyranny**!" he declared. In other words, if the American colonists could not have their own representatives in the British parliament, then Britain had no right to tax them. Americans from Maine to Georgia chanted Otis's words at protest meetings.

Patrick Henry, right, is shown addressing Virginia lawmakers in May 1765.

In Virginia, Patrick Henry made a fiery speech against the Stamp Act. On his twenty-ninth birthday—May 29, 1765—Henry arose in the Virginia legislature. "Caesar had his Brutus!" said Henry.

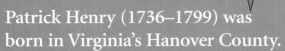

The Son of Thunder

Patrick Henry (1736–1799) was born in Virginia's Hanover County.

For a long time his life was pretty humble. As a young man he tended bar in his father-in-law's tavern, where he worked barefoot and wore old clothes. He also played the fiddle for the guests. Then, in his early twenties, he began to study law on his own.

At age twenty-four, Henry became a lawyer. A few years later, he was elected to Virginia's colonial legislature. Henry became known as a great speaker. He made his most famous speech in 1775 when he declared, "Give me liberty or give me death!"

Married twice, Patrick Henry had seventeen children and seventy grandchildren. In his old age, the Son of Thunder liked to dance around with his grandchildren as he played the fiddle.

"Charles the First his Cromwell! And George the Third—"

Henry's shocked colleagues reportedly ordered him to stop talking. Brutus killed Julius Caesar, a Roman ruler. Oliver Cromwell signed the death warrant for King Charles I of England. And George III was England's king at the time of the Stamp Act. Henry's fellow lawmakers were afraid Henry was about to say that George III should be murdered, too. If Henry said that, he might be arrested and charged with a serious crime called **treason**. Instead, he ended his sentence cleverly:

King George III (1738–1820)

"And George the Third," he said, "may profit by their example!"

Henry did not say that King George III should be murdered—yet he hinted as much. The power and anger in his speech thrilled American colonists. To many people, the man called the Son of Thunder embodied the growing spirit of **rebellion** in America.

Isaac Barre (1726–1802) was a British army officer and politician.

CHAPTER FOUR

The Sons of Liberty

The colonists were not alone in their protests against the Stamp Act. Some lawmakers in England believed their government was treating the colonists unfairly. Colonel Isaac Barre was one of them. Barre predicted that "those sons of **liberty**" across the Atlantic Ocean would fight the Stamp Act. The colonists thought that "sons of liberty" had a nice ring to it. In dozens of towns throughout the thirteen colonies, men formed groups called the Sons of Liberty.

The Sons of Liberty provided the muscle for the opposition to the Stamp Act. They held outdoor rallies under what they called liberty trees. They met indoors in what they called liberty halls. They also demonstrated—sometimes violently.

A 1765 cartoon shows a crowd bringing a bundle of wood and a gallows to hang and burn a dummy dressed as a British official.

One of the first Sons of Liberty groups was organized in New York City. New York's Sons held daily demonstrations against the Stamp Act. In the fall of 1765, they hanged and burned a dummy dressed as New York's British governor, Cadwallader Colden. This showed the Sons' dislike of British rule.

The British appointed officials to oversee the distribution of tax stamps in each colony. These men became the special targets of the Sons of Liberty. For example, a lawyer named Jared Ingersoll was assigned to distribute tax stamps in Connecticut. Five hundred Connecticut colonists, including many Sons of Liberty, captured Ingersoll as he was riding on horseback near Hartford. They waved clubs at him and forced him to quit his job as stamp master.

In South Carolina, a mob made up partly of Sons of Liberty forced two Stamp Act officials to quit their posts. New Jersey's Sons of Liberty also forced their colony's Stamp Act agent to quit. The most violent Stamp Act protests, however, took place in Boston, Massachusetts.

Sons and Daughters

During Revolutionary days, American women formed groups called the Daughters of Liberty. The Daughters refused to buy British clothing, tea, and other items. Instead, they made homespun clothing for their families. They gathered raspberries and mint leaves and made what they called liberty tea.

Bostonians took to the streets to riot and revel as outrage against the Stamp Act and British rule in general spread throughout the colonies.

CHAPTER FIVE

Boston's Stamp Act Riots

Samuel Adams was a main organizer of Boston's Sons of Liberty. Under Adams's direction, Boston's Sons marched through the streets as they shouted, "Liberty, property, and no stamps!"

In colonial times, destroying property was a very serious crime. Boston's Sons of Liberty did something shocking. In August 1765, they marched to the house of Andrew Oliver, who had accepted the job of stamp distributor in Massachusetts. The marchers threw stones through Oliver's windows, split open his front door with axes, and smashed his furniture. Later that August, they wrecked the house of Massachusetts lieutenant governor Thomas Hutchinson.

These house attacks were the main events in what would be called

The Master of the Puppets

Samuel Adams (1722–1803) was born in Boston. He graduated from nearby Harvard College. Unlike other Americans, Adams secretly liked the Stamp Act. By 1765, he was one of the first Americans to favor independence. He sought a reason for Americans to rebel against England, and the Stamp Act served the purpose.

During Revolutionary times, Adams wrote countless letters criticizing British rule. He signed them with false names—so it would appear that many people were complaining about the Mother Country —and sent them to newspapers.

The British hated Adams. They called him the Master of the Puppets because he told the Sons of Liberty what to do. Among other things, he planned the Boston Tea Party. Because he helped create the United States, Adams was nicknamed the Father of American Independence.

Sons of Liberty ransacked Governor Hutchinson's home on the night of August 26, 1765.

Boston's Stamp Act Riots. English officials were angry about the destruction, but they couldn't do anything about it. Jailing hundreds of rioters was impossible. Also, if British officials tried to arrest Adams and other ringleaders, the Sons of Liberty might destroy half of Boston.

James Otis (1725–1783), shown greeting a cheering crowd outside the Boston Town Hall, was one of America's leading rebels.

CHAPTER SIX

Congress Gathers to Fight

American leaders decided to work together to fight the Stamp Act. James Otis of Massachusetts suggested that **delegates** from all the colonies hold a meeting. Samuel Adams helped Otis organize this gathering. It was called the Stamp Act Congress.

The Stamp Act Congress opened in New York City's Federal Hall on October 7, 1765. Nine of the thirteen colonies sent delegates: Massachusetts, Connecticut, Rhode Island, New York, New Jersey, Pennsylvania, Delaware, Maryland, and South Carolina.

The Stamp Act Congress produced the **Declaration** of Rights and **Grievances**. One grievance was taxation without representation. Before the

Stamp Act Stars

The delegates of the Stamp Act Congress included some major figures of Revolutionary times. James Otis, planner of the **conference**, was from Massachusetts. Four other delegates would later sign the Declaration of Independence: Philip Livingston of New York, John Morton of Pennsylvania, and Thomas McKean and Caesar Rodney of Delaware. Three delegates were future signers of the U.S. Constitution: William Samuel Johnson of Connecticut, John Rutledge of South Carolina, and John Dickinson of Pennsylvania. South Carolina's Christopher Gadsden was one of the most passionate delegates. Later Gadsden would lead the fight for American independence in the **Continental Congress**.

Stamp Act Congress ended on October 25, 1765, delegates also produced a set of letters. The colonists mailed the letters to the two houses of the British parliament and to King George III. The letters requested that Parliament **repeal**, or cancel, the Stamp Act.

A week after the Stamp Act Congress ended, the new tax went into effect. Americans treated November 1, 1765, as a day of mourning. In Boston, church bells rang sadly. Ships in Boston Harbor flew their flags at half-mast, also as a sign of mourning.

In Portsmouth, New Hampshire, the Sons of Liberty held a mock funeral. They marched through the streets with a

New Hampshire colonists hang a dummy of a stamp agent during a demonstration against the Stamp Act.

coffin bearing the words LIBERTY—AGED 145. (It had been 145 years since the Pilgrims had landed at Plymouth Rock.) The Sons buried Miss Liberty in the ground. However, some colonists unearthed her when they claimed that they still heard her heart beating. Similar mock funerals were held for Miss Liberty in Rhode Island, Maryland, and North Carolina.

Colonists from all walks of life banded together in anger over the unfair tax imposed on them.

CHAPTER SEVEN

England's Huge Failure

The British were unable to **enforce** the Stamp Act. For one thing, the colonists had forced many Stamp Act officials to resign. For another, the Sons of Liberty threatened to punish anyone who cooperated with the tax law.

The Stamp Act did not raise the money that the Mother Country expected. Plus, it made the colonists extremely rebellious. To strike back at England, Americans began to **boycott**—refuse to buy—British goods. As a result, English merchants lost business and many English factory workers lost their jobs. These merchants and workers joined the Americans and asked for the Stamp Act to be repealed.

Protestors carry signs denouncing the British tax through the streets of New York City.

King George III and British lawmakers did not respond directly to the Stamp Act Congress's letters. They did not want to appear to be caving in to the Americans' demands. However, by early 1766 the British government was thinking about canceling the Stamp Act.

Giving in to the colonists was too bitter a pill for many British lawmakers to swallow. Parliament held heated debates over whether to repeal or enforce the Stamp Act. Finally, in early 1766, both houses of Parliament voted to repeal the Stamp Act. The king approved. On March 18, 1766, the Stamp Act was officially repealed.

The Stamp of Disapproval

Throughout the colonies, Americans closed their courthouses and offices rather than use the hated stamps. In twelve of the colonies, no tax stamps were sold. Georgia was the only colony that allowed tax stamps to be sold within its borders. Even in Georgia, however, few tax stamps were distributed.

A bellman rings the Liberty Bell to announce the repeal of the Stamp Act.

CHAPTER EIGHT

The Act That Sparked a War

In the spring of 1766, word of the Stamp Act's defeat reached America. Throughout the colonies people celebrated. They rang church bells—cheerfully this time. They also fired cannons and set off fireworks. Among the bells that rang in Philadelphia, Pennsylvania, was the Liberty Bell. Ten years later it would peal out the news of the Declaration of **Independence**.

Boston, Massachusetts, had the biggest celebrations. Musicians paraded through the streets while playing violins and flutes and banging on drums. Ships in the harbor fired their guns. The Liberty Tree was decorated with colorful streamers. That evening nearly every family in Boston lit candles and oil lamps and placed them in their windows. Boston turned into a city

This British cartoon depicts a mock funeral held to "bury" the failed Stamp Act after it was repealed.

of light. The Sons of Liberty launched fireworks in the field known as Boston Common.

The Stamp Act Riots had established Boston as the hotbed of the American rebellion. Later, most of the key events in the march to American independence would take place in and near Boston.

The Stamp Act was a turning point in U.S. history in several ways. To start with, the Stamp Act sparked serious conflict between the colonists and the British government. This clash grew more serious until it resulted in the creation of the United States a decade later.

The Stamp Act crisis also showed that Americans would no longer obey the Mother Country automatically. Instead, they would fight for their rights. Several American leaders entered the limelight. These leaders included Samuel Adams, John Dickinson, Caesar Rodney, and Patrick Henry. Their Stamp Act experiences would help them lead the nation during Revolutionary times.

Finally, the Stamp Act Congress taught the colonists that they could achieve great successes by banding together. It was a model for the Continental Congress, which later declared American independence.

Glossary

boycott—to refuse to do business with a person or organization

colonies—settlements that a country builds outside its borders

conference—a meeting or convention

Continental Congress—the body of lawmakers that governed the United States before the creation of the U.S. Congress

counterfeiting—the act of creating something that is a fake or an imitation

debt—something that is owed

declaration—an announcement

delegates—people who are assigned to go to a meeting to represent their community

enforce—to make people obey a rule or law

grievances—complaints

independence—freedom or self-government

liberty—freedom

parliament—a lawmaking body

rebellion—a revolt or expression of opposition to authority

repeal—to cancel something or bring it to an end

treason—a serious crime in which someone attempts to overthrow the government or to kill its leaders

tyranny—unjust or oppressive power

Timeline

1607—Virginia, the first of England's thirteen American colonies, is settled

1733—England establishes Georgia, its thirteenth and final American colony

1754–1763—With help from the American colonists, Britain wins the French and Indian War

1765—**March 22:** The Stamp Act is approved in Britain
October 7–25: Colonial leaders attend the Stamp Act Congress in New York City
November 1: The Stamp Act goes into effect

1607   *1733*   *1765*

1766—The Stamp Act is officially repealed on March 18; Parliament approves the Declaratory Act, which states the British government's right to make laws for the thirteen colonies "in all cases whatsoever"

1775—The Revolutionary War begins at Lexington, Massachusetts

1783—Americans win the Revolutionary War

1965—The United States observes the two hundredth anniversary of the Stamp Act

1766   *1775*   *1965*

Further Information

BOOKS

Anderson, Dale. *The Causes of the American Revolution.* Milwaukee: World Almanac Library, 2006.

Broida, Marian. *Projects About the American Revolution.* New York: Marshall Cavendish Benchmark, 2006.

Burgan, Michael. *The Stamp Act of 1765.* Minneapolis: Compass Point Books, 2005.

Fradin, Dennis Brindell. *Samuel Adams: The Father of American Independence.* New York: Clarion Books, 1998.

Laager, Hollie. *The French and Indian War.* Vero Beach, FL: Rourke Publishing, 2007.

Strum, Richard M. *Causes of the American Revolution.* Stockton, NJ: OTTN Publishing, 2005.

WEB SITES

For a brief description of the Stamp Act especially for kids:
http://www.socialstudiesforkids.com/wwww/us/stampactdef.htm

For a summary of the Stamp Act from Colonial Williamsburg, Virginia:
http://www.history.org/History/teaching/tchcrsta.cfm

For a short description of the Stamp Act era in New York from PBS Kids:
http://pbskids.org/bigapplehistory/ (Click on *Early New York*, then select *The Stamp Act* from the *Important Events* drop-down menu.)

For information on the Sons of Liberty in Boston and elsewhere:
http://www.ushistory.org/declaration/related/sons.htm

Bibliography

Labaree, Benjamin Woods. *Colonial Massachusetts: A History*. Millwood, NY: KTO Press, 1979.

Morgan, Edmund S., ed. *Prologue to Revolution: Sources and Documents on the Stamp Act Crisis, 1764–1766*. Chapel Hill: University of North Carolina Press, 1959.

Morgan, Edmund S., and Helen M. Morgan. *The Stamp Act Crisis: Prologue to Revolution*. Chapel Hill: University of North Carolina Press, 1953.

Tyler, Moses Coit. *Patrick Henry*. Boston and New York: Houghton Mifflin, 1887.

Wells, William V. *Life and Public Services of Samuel Adams*. Boston: Little, Brown, 1866. Reprint, Freeport, NY: Books for Libraries Press, 1969.

Weslager, C. A. *The Stamp Act Congress: With an Exact Copy of the Complete Journal*. Newark: University of Delaware Press, 1976.

Index

Page numbers in **boldface** are illustrations.

About the Author

Dennis Fradin is the author of 150 books, some of them written with his wife, Judith Bloom Fradin. Their book for Clarion, *The Power of One: Daisy Bates and the Little Rock Nine*, was named a Golden Kite Honor Book. Another of Dennis's well-known books is *Let It Begin Here! Lexington & Concord: First Battles of the American Revolution*, published by Walker. Other recent books by the Fradins include *Jane Addams: Champion of Democracy* for Clarion and *5,000 Miles to Freedom: Ellen and William Craft's Flight from Slavery* for National Geographic Children's Books. Their current project for National Geographic is the *Witness to Disaster* series about natural disasters. *Turning Points in U.S. History* is Dennis's first series for Marshall Cavendish Benchmark. The Fradins have three grown children and five grandchildren.